Soup Cookbook: Simple and He Recipes to Warm th

by **Vesela Tabakova**
Text copyright(c)2016 Vesela Tabakova
All Rights Reserved

Table Of Contents

Family-friendly Soups to Satisfy your Soul - and Stomach	5
Chicken Soup with Rice	6
Lemon Chicken and Kale Soup	7
Slow Cooker French-style Farmhouse Chicken Soup	8
Chicken Vegetable Soup	9
Slow Cooker Chicken Noodle Soup	10
Chicken and Ricotta Meatball Soup	11
Asparagus and Chicken Soup	12
Asian-style Chicken Soup	13
Smoked Meat Russian Soup	14
Bean, Chicken and Sausage Soup	16
Bulgarian Chicken Soup	17
Greek Lemon Chicken Soup	19
Mediterranean Chicken Soup	21
Turkish Chicken Soup	22
Moroccan Chicken and Butternut Squash Soup	23
Veal Tortellini Soup	25
Lamb Soup	26
Hearty Lamb and Vegetable Soup	28
Meatball and Chickpea Soup	29
Beef and Vegetable Minestrone	31
Beef Noodle Soup	33
Italian Wedding Soup	34
Lentil and Ground Beef Soup	36
Italian Meatball Soup	37
Bulgarian Meatball Soup	39
Easy Fish Soup	41
Spanish Seafood Soup	43
Italian Minestrone	45
Dump Bean and Bacon Soup	46
Fish and Noodle Soup	47
Lentil, Barley and Kale Soup	48
Spinach and Mushroom Soup	49
Simple Black Bean Soup	50
Bean and Pasta Soup	51

Lentil and Cabbage Soup	52
Creamy Zucchini Soup	53
Broccoli, Zucchini and Blue Cheese Soup	54
Beetroot and Carrot Soup	55
Baked Beet Soup	56
Borscht	58
Curried Parsnip Soup	59
Pumpkin and Bell Pepper Soup	60
Moroccan Pumpkin Soup	61
Spinach, Leek and Quinoa Soup	62
Vegetable Quinoa Soup	63
Broccoli and Potato Soup	64
Creamy Potato Soup	65
Leek, Rice and Potato Soup	66
Carrot and Chickpea Soup	67
Sweet Potato Soup	68
Irish Carrot Soup	69
Spicy Carrot Soup	70
Lentil, Barley and Mushroom Soup	71
Mushroom Soup	72
Mediterranean Chickpea Soup	73
French Vegetable Soup	74
Minted Pea Soup	75
Brown Lentil Soup	76
Moroccan Lentil Soup	77
White Bean Soup	78
Tomato Soup	79
Cauliflower Soup	80
Creamy Artichoke Soup	81
Tomato Artichoke Soup	82
Roasted Red Pepper Soup	83
Vietnamese Noodle Soup	84
Spinach, Nettle and Feta Cheese Soup	85
Nettle Soup	86
Gazpacho	87
Cold Cucumber Soup	88

FREE BONUS RECIPES: 20 Superfood Paleo and Vegan Smoothies for Vibrant Health and Easy Weight Loss	89
Winter Greens Smoothie	90
Delicious Kale Smoothie	91
Cherry Smoothie	92
Banana and Coconut Smoothie	93
Avocado and Pineapple Smoothie	94
Carrot and Mango Smoothie	95
Strawberry and Coconut Smoothie	96
Beautiful Skin Smoothie	97
Kiwi and Pear Smoothie	98
Tropical Smoothie	99
Melon Smoothie	100
Healthy Skin Smoothie	101
Paleo Dessert Smoothie	102
Easy Superfood Smoothie	103
Antioxidant Smoothie	104
Coconut and Date Smoothie	105
Kiwi and Grapefruit Smoothie	106
Mango and Nectarine Smoothie	107
Pineapple Smoothie	108
Easy Vitamin Smoothie	109
About the Author	110

Family-friendly Soups to Satisfy your Soul - and Stomach

Soup, glorious soup! I love it and can happily eat it every day. Soup is filling, soup is warming, soup is healthy, and soup is comforting. Homemade soup is diet friendly, it curbs cravings and prevents overeating.

You can have soup for lunch, dinner, and even for breakfast. You can eat it in fall and winter, but you can also eat it in summer, especially delicious cold soups as the cold yogurt soup, or Spanish gazpacho.

Most of my soup recipes come from my mother's and grandmother's personal collections of recipes. Some are the original recipes which still work beautifully today, some I have adapted to suit my family's - particularly my teenage kids' 21st century taste buds.

Homemade soups are inexpensive and taste so much nicer than many ready-made ones. Soup is easy and versatile, it is also adaptable - you can always improvise and use whatever ingredients you have at home.

Weeknight dinner ideas are hard to come by. For me, preparing delicious homemade soups is the easiest stress-free way of cooking healthy, yet amazingly tasty food for the family. My favorite soup recipes use simple ingredients that you probably already have in your freezer, refrigerator, and pantry. They do not require complicated cooking techniques and are simply the best solution for fast-paced families who want tasty and healthy meals. At the end of a busy day a steaming bowl of soup is the perfect answer to the question 'What's for dinner?'

Chicken Soup with Rice

Serves 4

Ingredients:

1 lb boneless chicken thighs, cut in bite sized pieces

1/4 cup rice, rinsed

1 small onion, finely cut

2 carrots, grated

1 celery rib, finely cut

5 cups water

2 garlic cloves, chopped

1 bay leaf

1 tsp salt

1/2 tsp black pepper

1/2 cup fresh parsley, finely cut, to serve

4 tbsp lemon juice, to serve

Directions:

Heat a soup pot over medium heat. Gently sauté onion, garlic, carrot and celery, stirring occasionally.

Add in chicken, water and bay leaf and bring to a boil. Simmer for 10 minutes then season with salt and black pepper and add in rice. Stir to combine and simmer for 15 minutes more. Remove the bay leaf and serve with parsley and lemon juice.

Lemon Chicken and Kale Soup

Serves 5-6

Ingredients:

1 cup cooked chicken, cubed or shredded

1 small onion, chopped

1 small carrot, grated

1 bunch kale, cut into 1 inch pieces

4 cups chicken broth

1 tsp Worcestershire sauce

1 tsp Dijon mustard

3 tbsp olive oil

1 tsp paprika

3 tbsp lemon juice

1 tsp grated lemon zest

salt and black pepper, to taste

grated Parmesan cheese, to serve

Directions:

Heat a soup pot over medium heat. Gently sauté onion, garlic and carrot, stirring occasionally. Stir in the lemon zest, chicken broth, Worcestershire sauce, Dijon mustard and cooked chicken.

Bring to a boil then reduce heat and simmer for 10 minutes. Stir in the kale and simmer for 3-4 minutes or until kale is tender.

Stir in the lemon juice and season with salt and pepper to taste. Serve sprinkled with Parmesan cheese.

Slow Cooker French-style Farmhouse Chicken Soup

Serves 5-6

Ingredients:

4 skinless, boneless chicken thighs, cut into bite-sized pieces

1 leek, trimmed, halved, finely cut

1 celery rib, trimmed, halved, finely cut

2 carrots, chopped

1 fennel bulb, trimmed, diced

1 cup frozen peas

4 cups chicken broth

1 tsp thyme

1 tsp salt

Directions:

Combine all ingredients in the slow cooker.

Cover and cook on low for 6-7 hours.

Chicken Vegetable Soup

Serves 6-7

Ingredients:

2 lb boneless chicken thighs, cut in bite sized pieces

1 small onion, chopped

1 celery rib, chopped

1/2 small parsnip, chopped

3 garlic cloves, chopped

1 carrot, chopped

1 red bell pepper, chopped

1 lb potatoes, peeled and cubed

5 cups chicken broth

1 tsp thyme

2 bay leaves

1 tsp salt

black pepper, to taste

1 tsp summer savory

Directions:

Season the chicken well with salt, ground black pepper and summer savory. Place it in a slow cooker with all remaining ingredients.

Cover and cook on low for 6-7 hours or on high for 4 hours.

Slow Cooker Chicken Noodle Soup

Serves 6-7

Ingredients:

2 lb boneless chicken thighs, cut in bite sized pieces

1 small onion, chopped

1 tomato, diced

1 red bell pepper, chopped

2-3 broccoli florets

4 cups chicken broth

2 cups wide egg noodles, uncooked

1 tsp garlic powder

1 tsp oregano

2 bay leaves

1 tsp salt

black pepper, to taste

Directions:

Season the chicken well with salt, black pepper garlic powder and oregano. Place it in a slow cooker with all remaining ingredients.

Cover and cook on low for 6-7 hours or on high for 4-5 hours.

Add noodles to slow cooker; cover and cook on low 20 minutes.

Chicken and Ricotta Meatball Soup

Serves 4-5

Ingredients:

1 lb ground chicken meat

1 egg, lightly whisked

1 cup whole milk ricotta

1 cup grated Parmesan cheese

2-3 tbsp flour

1/2 onion, chopped

4 cups chicken broth

2 cups baby spinach

1/2 tsp dried oregano

3 tbsp olive oil

½ tsp black pepper

Directions:

Place ground chicken, Ricotta, Parmesan, egg and black pepper in a bowl. Combine well with hands and roll teaspoonfuls of the mixture into balls. Roll each meatball in the flour then set aside on a large plate.

In a deep soup pot, heat olive oil and gently sauté onion until transparent. Add in oregano and chicken broth and bring to a boil. Add meatballs, reduce heat, and simmer, uncovered, for 15 minutes.

Add baby spinach leaves and simmer for 2 more minutes until it wilts.

Asparagus and Chicken Soup

Serves 4

Ingredients:

5 cups chicken broth

2 leeks, finely cut

2 chicken breast fillets, cooked and shredded

1 bunch asparagus, trimmed and cut

1/2 cup parsley, finely chopped

salt and black pepper, to taste

lemon juice, to serve

Directions:

Heat the chicken broth in a large soup pot. Add in the shredded chicken and the leeks and bring to the boil.

Reduce heat and simmer for 5 minutes. Add the asparagus, parsley, salt and black pepper and cook for 2 minutes more. Serve with lemon juice.

Asian-style Chicken Soup

Serves 4-5

Ingredients:

1 roasted chicken, skin and bones removed, shredded

1/2 Chinese cabbage, shredded

5 cups chicken broth

1 cup water

1 red chili, thinly sliced

2 carrots, peeled and cut into short, thin sticks

4 oz fresh shiitake mushrooms, sliced

16 oz snow peas, shredded lengthwise

2 tbsp soy sauce

1/4 cup coriander leaves, finely cut

Directions:

Combine the chicken broth, water, soy sauce and the chilli in a deep soup pot. Gently bring to a boil then add in carrots, mushrooms, snow peas and shredded chicken.

Reduce heat and simmer for 3-4 minutes. Add the cabbage and cook for 2 minutes or until the cabbage wilts. Stir the coriander into soup. Divide soup between bowls and serve.

Smoked Meat Russian Soup

Serves 4

Ingredients:

3 cups chicken broth

2 cups water

1 onion, finely cut

1 large potato, diced

1 large carrot, grated

2 oz bacon, chopped

3 oz smoked pork sausage, chopped

5 oz smoked chicken breast, cubed

2 pickled cucumbers, chopped

3 tbsp tomato purée

1 tsp paprika

lemon juice, to serve

black olives, chopped, to serve

finely chopped parsnip, to serve

black pepper, to serve

Directions:

Combine the chicken broth and water in a deep soup pot and slowly bring to the boil.

In a deep frying pan, cook sausage, bacon and chicken breast for 3-4 minutes, then add in onion and carrot and cook for 2-3 minutes more, stirring constantly. Add in chopped pickled cucumbers, stir, and cook for 5 minutes. Add tomato purée and paprika, stir, and remove from heat.

Cut the potato and add it to the boiling broth. Let it simmer for 5 minutes then add in the fried meat and all other ingredients. Cook on low heat for 10 minutes then serve sprinkled with chopped olives, parsnip and lemon juice.

Bean, Chicken and Sausage Soup

Serves 6-7

Ingredients:

12 oz Italian sausage

3 bacon strips, diced

2 cups chicken, cooked and cut in small pieces

1 cup kidney beans, rinsed and drained

1 big onion, chopped

2 garlic cloves, crushed

4 cups water

1 cup canned tomatoes, diced, undrained

1 bay leaf

1 tsp dried thyme

1 tsp savory

½ tsp dried basil

salt and pepper, to taste

Directions:

Cook the sausage, onion and bacon over medium heat until the sausage is no longer pink. Drain off the fat. Add the garlic and cook for a minute. Add in the water, tomatoes and seasonings and bring to a boil.

Cover, reduce heat and simmer for 30 minutes. Add the chicken and beans. Simmer for 5 minutes. Serve warm.

Bulgarian Chicken Soup

Serves 7-8

Ingredients:

1 whole chicken, cut into sections

1 large onion, whole

1 large onion, chopped

3 garlic cloves, chopped

2 carrots, chopped

1 red pepper

1 tsp thyme

2 bay leaves

2 tbsp olive oil

1 tsp salt

black pepper to taste

1 tbsp fresh oregano, chopped

1 tsp summer savory

Directions:

Place the chicken, bay leaves, salt, whole onion and whole red pepper into a pot with 5 cups of cold water. Bring the pot to boil, reduce heat and simmer for 1 hour, scooping out any solid foam that settles at the top.

When ready, strain the broth and reserve. Remove the meat from the chicken and cut into large chunks. Discard the bay leaves, the onion and the pepper.

Place the pot back on the stove, sauté the other onion, garlic, carrots and thyme for about 5 minutes. Pour in the broth and season with salt and pepper.

Simmer for about 20 minutes or until the vegetables are tender. Add in the chicken pieces, the savory and the oregano.

Simmer for 10 more minutes and serve warm.

Greek Lemon Chicken Soup

Serves 4-5

Ingredients:

1 lb uncooked boneless, skinless chicken breast, diced

1/3 cup rice

4 cups chicken broth

1 cup water

1 onion, finely diced

2 large raw eggs

3 tbsp olive oil

1/2 cup fresh lemon juice

1 tsp salt

1 tsp ground pepper

a bunch of fresh parsley for garnish, finely cut

Directions:

In a medium pot, heat the olive oil and sauté the onions until they are soft and translucent. Add the chicken broth and water, along with the washed rice and bring everything to boil, then reduce heat.

When the rice is almost done, add the diced chicken breast to the pot. Let it cook for another 5 minutes or until the chicken is cooked through.

In a small bowl, beat the eggs and lemon juice together. Pour two cups of broth slowly into the egg mixture, whisking constantly. When all the broth is incorporated, add this mixture into the pot of chicken soup and stir well to blend.

Do not boil any more. Season with salt and pepper and garnish with parsley. Serve hot.

Mediterranean Chicken Soup

Serves 6-8

Ingredients:

about 1.5 lb chicken breasts

3-4 carrots, chopped

1 celery rib, chopped

1 red onion, chopped

1/3 cup rice

6 cups water

10 black olives, pitted and halved

fresh parsley or coriander, to serve

1/2 tsp salt

ground black pepper, to taste

lemon juice, to serve

Directions:

Place the chicken breasts in a soup pot. Add in onion, carrots, celery, salt, black pepper and water. Stir well and bring to a boil. Add in rice and olives, stir, and reduce heat. Simmer for 30 minutes.

Remove chicken from the pot and let it cool slightly. Shred it and return it back to the pot. Serve soup with lemon juice and sprinkled with fresh parsley or coriander.

Turkish Chicken Soup

Serves 6

Ingredients:

about 1.5 lb chicken breasts

4 tbsp butter

3 tbsp flour

3 cups of milk

4 cups water

1 tsp paprika

salt and ground black pepper, to taste

Directions:

Boil the chicken breasts in 4 cups of water for 30 minutes or until cooked through. Remove chicken from the soup pot and leave it in a plate to cool. When cool enough shred and leave it aside.

Melt one tablespoon of butter with three tablespoons of flour in a small pan. Mix flour and butter well and cook until the mixture begins to brown, then remove from heat.

Bring the chicken broth to a boil. Strain the flour and butter mixture in a strainer and stir into the soup. Add the shredded chicken and 3-4 cups of milk (depending on how thick you want the soup). Bring to the boil again and simmer for 5 minutes. Remove from heat.

In another pan melt three tablespoons of butter. Add in paprika and a teaspoon of dried mint and fry for a minute. Pour butter mixture over the soup and serve hot.

Moroccan Chicken and Butternut Squash Soup

Serves 7-8

Ingredients:

3 skinless, boneless chicken thighs (about 14 oz), cut into bite-sized pieces

1 big onion, chopped

1 zucchini, quartered lengthwise and sliced into 1/2 inch pieces

3 cups peeled butternut squash, cut in 1/2 inch pieces

2 tbsp tomato paste

4 cups chicken broth

1/3 cup uncooked couscous

1/2 tsp ground cumin

1/4 teaspoon ground cinnamon

1 tsp paprika

1 tsp salt

2 tbsp fresh basil leaves, chopped

1 tbsp grated orange rind

3 tbsp olive oil

Directions:

Heat a soup pot over medium heat. Gently sauté onion, for 3-4 minutes, stirring occasionally. Add in chicken and cook for 4-5 minutes until chicken is brown on all sides. Add cumin, cinnamon and paprika and stir well.

Add butternut squash and tomato paste; stir again. Add in chicken broth and bring to a boil, then reduce heat and simmer for 10 minutes. Stir in couscous, salt and zucchini pieces; cook until squash is tender. Remove pot from heat. Season with salt and pepper to taste. Stir in chopped basil and orange rind and serve.

Veal Tortellini Soup

Serves 4

Ingredients:

4 cups beef broth

3 cups tomato passata

1 tsp sugar

12 oz veal or beef tortellini

black pepper, to taste

1 tbsp dry basil,

1/2 cup parsley, finely cut

Directions:

Place the beef broth, tomato passata, sugar, salt and pepper in a large saucepan over medium heat and bring to a boil.

Add the tortellini and cook following packet instructions or until al dente.

Divide the tortellini among serving bowls and pour over the soup. Sprinkle with basil and serve hot.

Lamb Soup

Serves 5-6

Ingredients:

2 lbs lean boneless lamb, cubed

1 onion, finely cut

1 carrot, chopped

10 spring onions, chopped

2 tomato, diced

4 cups hot water

2 tbsp olive oil

1/2 tsp paprika

1 tsp salt

black pepper, to taste

1 tbsp dry mint

1/2 cup parsley, finely cut

2 eggs

Directions:

Heat 2 tablespoonfuls of olive oil and gently brown the lamb cubes in a medium sized cooking pot. Add the finely cut onion and the carrot and sauté for a minute or two, stirring. Add paprika and two cups of hot water.

Bring to the boil, then lower heat to medium-low and simmer until the lamb softens. Add in 2 more cups of hot water, spring onions, tomato, mint, salt and black pepper. Bring to a boil again and simmer for 10 minutes.

Whisk the the eggs in a small bowl. Take one ladle from the soup and add into the egg mixture, whisk. Take another and whisk again. Pour this mixture back into into the soup and stir. Do not boil. Sprinkle with parsley and serve while still hot.

Hearty Lamb and Vegetable Soup

Serves 6-7

Ingredients:

2 cups roasted lamb, shredded

3 cups chicken or vegetable broth

1 cup water

1 cup canned tomatoes, diced, undrained

1 onion, chopped

1 large carrot, chopped

1 small turnip, chopped

1 celery rib

3 tbsp olive oil

salt and black pepper, to taste

Directions:

Gently heat olive oil in a large saucepan and sauté onion, carrot, celery and turnip, stirring, for 5 minutes, or until softened.

Add in lamb, broth, tomatoes, and a cup of water. Bring to the boil then reduce heat and simmer for 20 minutes, or until vegetables are tender.

Season with salt and black pepper to taste.

Meatball and Chickpea Soup

Serves 4-5

Ingredients:

1 lb lean ground beef

3-4 tbsp flour

1 small onion, chopped

1 garlic clove, chopped

1 can tomatoes, diced and undrained

1 can chickpeas, drained

1 green pepper, chopped

4 cups water

½ bunch of parsley, finely cut

3 tbsp olive oil

½ tsp black pepper

1 tsp dried mint

1 tsp paprika

1 tsp salt

Directions:

Combine ground meat, paprika, black pepper and salt in a large bowl. Mix well with hands and roll teaspoonfuls of the mixture into balls. Put flour in a small bowl and roll each meatball in the flour, coating entire surface then set aside on a large plate.

Heat olive oil into a large soup pot and gently sauté onion, garlic and pepper until tender.

Add water and tomatoes and bring to the boil over high heat. Add in meatballs and chickpeas.

Reduce heat to low and simmer, uncovered, for 25 minutes. Add mint and stir. Serve with lemon juice.

Beef and Vegetable Minestrone

Serves 7-8

Ingredients:

2 slices bacon, chopped

1 cup lean ground beef

2 carrots, chopped

2 cloves garlic, finely chopped

1 large onion, chopped

1 celery rib, chopped

1 bay leaf

1 tsp dried basil

1 tsp dried rosemary, crushed

1/4 tsp crushed chillies

1 cup canned tomatoes, chopped

4 cups beef broth

1 cup canned chickpeas, drained

½ cup small pasta

Directions:

In a large saucepan, cook bacon and ground beef until well done, breaking up the beef as it cooks. Drain off the fat and add carrots, garlic, onion and celery.

Cook for about 5 minutes, or until the onions are translucent. Season with the bay leaf, basil, rosemary and crushed chillies. Stir in tomatoes and beef broth.

Bring to a boil then reduce heat and simmer for about 20 minutes. Add the chickpeas and pasta. Cook uncovered, for about 10 minutes or until the pasta is ready.

Beef Noodle Soup

Serves 7-8

Ingredients:

8 oz fillet steak, thinly sliced

6 oz rice stick noodles

2 carrots, peeled, halved, sliced diagonally

1 red pepper, deseeded, thinly sliced diagonally

7-8 spring onions, chopped

8 oz green beans, sliced diagonally

3 tbsp sweet chilli sauce

4 cups beef broth

1 tbsp olive oil

Directions:

In a skillet, heat olive oil and cook beef, stirring, until medium rare.

Place broth and half the onions in a saucepan over high heat. Bring to the boil, cover, reduce heat to low. Simmer for 5 minutes then add carrots, pepper and beans. Bring to the boil, uncovered. Cook for 2 minutes or until vegetables are tender. Remove from heat.

Stir in remaining onions and sweet chilli sauce.

Place noodles in a heatproof bowl. Cover with boiling water. Stand for 5 minutes or until tender. Drain. Divide noodles between bowls. Top with beef. Ladle over boiling soup mixture. Serve.

Italian Wedding Soup

Serves 4-5

Ingredients:

1 lb lean ground beef

1/3 cup breadcrumbs

1 egg, lightly beaten

1 onion, grated

2 carrots, chopped

1 small head escarole, trimmed and cut into 1/2 inch strips

1 cup baby spinach leaves

1 cup small pasta

2 tbsp Parmesan cheese, grated

2 tbsp parsley, finely cut

1 tsp salt

1 tsp ground black pepper

3 tbsp olive oil

3 cups chicken broth

3 cups water

1 tsp dried oregano

Directions:

Combine ground beef, egg, onion, breadcrumbs, cheese, parsley, 1/2 teaspoon of the salt and 1/2 teaspoon of the black pepper. Mix well with hands. Using a tablespoon, make walnut sized meatballs.

Heat olive oil in a large skillet and brown meatballs in batches.

Place aside on a plate.

In a large soup pot boil broth and water together with carrots, oregano, and the remaining salt and pepper. Gently add meatballs.

Reduce heat and simmer for 30 minutes. Add pasta, spinach and escarole and simmer 10 minutes more.

Lentil and Ground Beef Soup

Serves 6

Ingredients:

1 lb ground beef

1 cup brown lentils

2 carrots, chopped

2 onions, chopped

1 potato, cut into 1/2 inch cubes

4 garlic cloves, chopped

2 tomatoes, grated or pureed

5 cups water

1 tsp summer savory

1 tsp oregano

1 tsp paprika

2 tbsp olive oil

1 tsp salt

ground black pepper, to taste

Directions:

Heat olive oil in a large soup pot. Brown beef, breaking it up with a spoon. Add paprika and garlic and stir. Add lentils, remaining vegetables, water and spice.

Bring to a boil. Reduce heat to low and simmer, covered, for about an hour, or until lentils are tender. Stir occasionally.

Italian Meatball Soup

Serves 6-7

Ingredients:

1 lb lean ground beef

1 small onion, grated

1 onion, chopped

2 garlic cloves, crushed

½ cup breadcrumbs

3-4 basil leaves, finely chopped

1/3 cup Parmesan cheese, grated

1 egg, lightly beaten

2 cups tomato sauce with basil

3 cups water

½ cup small pasta

1 zucchini, diced

½ cup green beans, trimmed, cut into thirds

2 tbsp olive oil

Directions:

Combine ground meat, grated onion, garlic, breadcrumbs, basil, Parmesan and egg in a large bowl. Season with salt and pepper. Mix well with hands and roll tablespoonfuls of the mixture into balls. Place on a large plate.

Heat olive oil into a large deep saucepan and sauté onion and garlic until transparent. Add tomato sauce, water, and bring to the boil over high heat. Add meatballs.

Reduce heat to medium-low and simmer, uncovered, for 10 minutes. Add in pasta and cook for 5 more minutes.

Add the zucchini and beans. Cook until pasta and vegetables are tender. Serve sprinkled with Parmesan.

Bulgarian Meatball Soup

Serves 7-8

Ingredients:

1 lb lean ground beef

3-4 tbsp flour

1 onion, chopped

2 garlic cloves, cut

1 tomato, diced

2 potatoes, diced

1 green pepper, chopped

4 cups water

5.5 oz vermicelli, broken into pieces

½ bunch of parsley, finely cut

3 tbsp olive oil

½ tsp black pepper

1 tsp summer savory

1 tsp paprika

1 tsp salt

Directions:

Combine ground meat, savory, paprika, black pepper and salt in a large bowl. Mix well with hands and roll teaspoonfuls of the mixture into balls. Put flour in a small bowl and roll each meatball in the flour, coating entire surface then set aside on a large plate.

Heat olive oil into a large soup pot and sauté onion and garlic until transparent. Add water and bring to the boil over high heat. Add meatballs, carrot, green pepper and potatoes.

Reduce heat to low and simmer, uncovered, for 15 minutes. Add tomato, parsley and vermicelli and cook for 5 more minutes.

Serve with a dollop of yogurt on top.

Easy Fish Soup

Serves 6-7

Ingredients:

1 lb white fish fillets cut in small pieces

9 oz scallops

1 onion, chopped

4 tomatoes, chopped

3 potatoes, diced

1 red pepper, chopped

2 carrots, diced

1 garlic clove, crushed

a bunch of fresh parsley

3 tbsp olive oil

a pinch of cayenne pepper

1 tsp dried oregano

1 tsp dried thyme

1 tsp dried dill

½ tsp pepper

½ cup white wine

4 cups water

1/3 cup heavy cream

Directions:

Heat the olive oil over medium heat and sauté the onion, red pepper, garlic and carrots until tender. Stir in the cayenne, herbs, salt, and pepper. Add the white wine, water, potatoes and tomatoes and bring to a boil.

Reduce heat, cover, and cook until the potatoes are almost done. Stir in the fish and the scallops and cook for another 10 minutes. Stir in the heavy cream and parsley and serve hot.

Spanish Seafood Soup

Serves 8-9

Ingredients:

2 lb whole raw prawns

3 cups cold water

3 spring onions, chopped

1 bell pepper, finely chopped

2 large tomatoes, diced

1 tbsp tomato puree

2 garlic cloves, crushed

2 tbsp olive oil

2 bay leaves

1 tsp paprika

½ tsp cayenne pepper

salt and pepper, to taste

the juice of one small lemon

a bunch of parsley, chopped

Directions:

De-head and de-shell the prawns and leave them in a bowl to the side. Put the heads and shells in a pan with cold water. Add the bay leaves, bring to the boil and reduce heat. Simmer for 20 minutes.

While the broth is simmering sauté the shallots and pepper in olive oil for 5 minutes, then add the garlic for two more minutes. When the broth is ready strain it and add it to the the shallots.

Bring to the boil, add the tomatoes and tomato puree, the prawns, the mussels and simmer for 10 more minutes.

When the soup is ready, add the paprika and cayenne pepper, season to taste with salt and pepper and add the lemon juice. Garnish with parsley and serve.

Italian Minestrone

Serves 6-7

Ingredients:

1 cup cabbage, chopped

2 carrots, chopped

1 celery rib, thinly sliced

1 small onion, chopped

2 garlic cloves, chopped

1 tbsp olive oil

5 cups water

1 cup canned tomatoes, diced, undrained

1 cup fresh spinach, torn

½ cup pasta, cooked

black pepper and salt, to taste

Directions:

Sauté carrots, cabbage, celery, onion and garlic in oil for 5 minutes in a deep saucepan. Add water and tomatoes and bring to a boil.

Reduce heat and simmer uncovered, for 20 minutes or until vegetables are tender.

Stir in spinach, macaroni and season with black pepper and salt to taste.

Dump Bean and Bacon Soup

Serves 5-6

Ingredients:

1 slices bacon, chopped

1 can Black Beans, rinsed

1 can Kidney Beans, rinsed

1 celery rib, chopped

1/2 red onion, chopped

1 can tomatoes, diced, undrained

4 cups water

1 tsp smoked paprika

1 tsp dried mint

1/2 cup fresh parsley

ground black pepper, to taste

Directions:

Dump all ingredients in a soup pot. Stir well and bring to a boil. Reduce heat and simmer for 35 minutes.

Season with salt and black pepper to taste, and serve.

Fish and Noodle Soup

Serves 4-5

Ingredients:

14 oz firm white fish, cut into strips

2 carrots, cut into ribbons

1 zucchini, cut into thin ribbons

7 oz white button mushrooms, sliced

1 celery rib, finely cut

1 cup baby spinach

7 oz fresh noodles

3 cups chicken broth

2 cups water

2 tbsp soy sauce

1/2 tsp ground ginger

black pepper, to taste

Directions:

Place chicken broth, water and soy sauce in a large saucepan. Bring to a boil and add in carrots, celery, zucchini, mushrooms, ginger and noodles.

Cook, partially covered, for 3-4 minutes then add in fish and simmer for 3 minutes or until the fish is cooked through. Add baby spinach and simmer, stirring, for 1 minute, or until it wilts. Season with

black pepper and serve.

Lentil, Barley and Kale Soup

Serves 4

Ingredients:

2 medium leeks, chopped

2 garlic cloves, chopped

2 bay leaves

1 can tomatoes, diced and undrained

1/2 cup red lentils

1/2 cup barley

1 bunch kale, coarsely chopped

4 cups vegetable broth

3 tbsp olive oil

1 tbsp paprika

½ tsp cumin

Directions:

Heat olive oil in a large saucepan over medium-high heat and sauté leeks and garlic until fragrant. Add in cumin, paprika, tomatoes, lentils, barley and vegetable broth. Season with salt and pepper.

Cover, and bring to a boil then reduce heat and simmer for 40 minutes or until barley is tender.

Add in kale and let it simmer for a few minutes more until it wilts.

Spinach and Mushroom Soup

Serves 4-5

Ingredients:

1 small onion, finely cut

1 small carrot, chopped

1 small zucchini, peeled and diced

1 medium potato, peeled and diced

6-7 white button mushrooms, chopped

2 cups chopped fresh spinach

4 cups vegetable broth or water

4 tbsp olive oil

salt and black pepper, to taste

Directions:

Heat olive oil in a large soup pot over medium heat. Add in potato, onion and mushroom and cook until vegetables are soft but not mushy.

Add chopped fresh spinach, the zucchini and vegetable broth and simmer for about 15 minutes. Season to taste with salt and pepper and serve.

Simple Black Bean Soup

Serves 5-6

Ingredients:

1 cup dried black beans

5 cups vegetable broth

1 large onion, chopped

1 red pepper, chopped

1 tsp sweet paprika

1 tbsp dried mint

2 bay leaves

1 Serrano chili, finely chopped

1 tsp salt

4 tbsp fresh lime juice

1/2 cup chopped fresh cilantro

1 cup sour cream or yogurt, to serve

Directions:

Wash the beans and soak them in enough water overnight.

In a slow cooker, combine the beans and all other ingredients except for the lime juice and cilantro. Cover and cook on low for 7-8 hours.

Add salt, lime juice and fresh cilantro.

Serve with a dollop of sour cream or yogurt.

Bean and Pasta Soup

Serves 6-7

Ingredients:

1 cup small pasta, cooked

1 cup canned white kidney beans, rinsed and drained

2 medium carrots, thinly sliced

1 cup fresh spinach, torn

1 medium onion, chopped

1 celery rib, thinly sliced

2 garlic cloves, crushed

3 cups water

1 cup canned tomatoes, diced and undrained

1 cup vegetable broth

½ tsp dried rosemary

½ tsp dried basil

2 tbsp olive oil

salt and pepper, to taste

Directions:

Heat the olive oil over medium heat and sauté the onion, carrots and celery. Add the garlic and cook for a minute longer. Stir in the water, tomatoes, vegetable broth, basil, rosemary, salt and pepper.

Bring to a boil then reduce heat and simmer for 10 minutes, or until the carrots are tender. Drain pasta and add it to the vegetables. Add the beans and spinach and cook until spinach is wilted.

Lentil and Cabbage Soup

Serves 6-7

Ingredients:

1 cup dry lentils

1/2 onion, finely cut

2 carrots, cut

1 celery rib, chopped

1/2 head cabbage, sliced

2 garlic cloves, crushed

3 cups vegetable broth

1 cup water

2 tbsp olive oil

1 tbsp savory

1 tsp paprika

salt and pepper, to taste

Directions:

In a large soup pot, heat olive oil over medium-high heat and gently sauté onion and garlic for a minute or two. Add in celery, carrots and cook for an addition 2 minutes.

Once the onion is tender, add paprika, savory, dry lentils and stir well. Stir in 3 cups of vegetable broth, and 1 cup water.

Bring the soup to a boil, add cabbage, lower heat, and simmer for about 30-40 minutes, or until the cabbage is tender.

Creamy Zucchini Soup

Serves 4

Ingredients:

1 onion, finely chopped

2 garlic cloves, crushed

1 cup vegetable broth

3 cups water

5 zucchinis, peeled, thinly sliced

1 big potato, chopped

1/4 cup fresh basil leaves

1 tsp sugar

½ cup yogurt, to serve

Parmesan cheese, to serve

Directions:

Heat oil in a saucepan over medium heat and sauté the onion and garlic, stirring, for 2-3 minutes or until soft.

Add the vegetable broth and water and bring to the boil, then reduce heat to medium-low. Add in zucchinis, the potato, a teaspoon of sugar and simmer, stirring occasionally, for 10 minutes, or until the zucchinis are soft.

Stir in basil and simmer for 2-3 minutes. Set aside to cool then blend in batches and reheat soup. Serve with a dollop of yogurt and/or sprinkled with Parmesan cheese.

Broccoli, Zucchini and Blue Cheese Soup

Serves 4-5

Ingredients:

2 leeks, white part only, sliced

1 head broccoli, coarsely chopped

2 zucchinis, chopped

1 potato, chopped

2 cups vegetable broth

3 cups water

3 tbsp olive oil

3.5 oz blue cheese, crumbled

1/3 cup light cream

Directions:

Heat the oil in a large saucepan over medium heat. Sauté the leeks, stirring, for 5 minutes or until soft. Add bite sized pieces of broccoli, zucchinis, potato, water and broth and bring to a boil.

Reduce heat to low and simmer, stirring occasionally, for 10 minutes, or until vegetables are just tender. Remove from heat and set aside for 5 minutes to cool slightly.

Transfer soup to a blender. Add the cheese and blend in batches until smooth. Return to saucepan and place over low heat. Add cream and stir to combine. Season with salt and pepper to taste.

Beetroot and Carrot Soup

Serves 6

Ingredients:

4 beets, washed and peeled

2 carrots, peeled, chopped

2 potatoes, peeled, chopped

1 medium onion, chopped

2 cups vegetable broth

3 cups water

2 tbsp yogurt

2 tbsp olive oil

a bunch or spring onions, finely cut, to serve

Directions:

Peel and chop the beets. Heat the olive oil in a saucepan over medium high heat and sauté the onion and carrot until the onion is tender. Add in beets, potatoes, broth and water.

Bring to the boil. Reduce heat to medium and simmer, partially covered, for 30-40 minutes, or until the beets are tender. Cool slightly.

Blend the soup in batches until smooth. Return it to pan over low heat and cook, stirring, for 4-5 minutes or until heated through. Season with salt and pepper. Serve soup topped with yogurt and sprinkled with spring onions.

Baked Beet Soup

Serves 6

Ingredients:

1.5 lb fresh beets, peeled, grated

2 carrots, chopped

1 onion, chopped

2 apples, peeled and chopped

1 tbsp sugar

1 bay leaf

2 tbs lemon juice

3 cups vegetable broth

2 cups water

3 tbsp olive oil

1 cup heavy cream

a bunch of fresh parsley, chopped, to serve

Directions:

Preheat the oven to 350 F. Toss the beets, apples, onion and carrots in olive oil and arrange in a casserole dish. Add the bay leaf, vegetable broth and water.

Season with salt and pepper, cover with foil and bake for 1-2 hours. Discard the bay leaf and set aside to cool. Blend everything in a blender, in batches, until smooth, then transfer to a large saucepan.

Season with salt and pepper to taste, stir in the cream and reheat without boiling. Serve the soup with a dollop of extra cream and sprinkled with chopped parsley.

Borscht

Serves 6

Ingredients:

4 beets, peeled, quartered

1 carrot, peeled, chopped

1 parsnip, peeled, cut into chunks

1 leek, white part only, sliced

1 onion, chopped

1/3 cup lemon juice

½ tsp nutmeg

3 bay leaves

6 cups vegetable broth

1 cup sour cream

2-3 tbsp finely cut dill, to serve

Directions:

Place the beets, carrot, parsnip, leek, onion, lemon juice, spices and bay leaves in a large saucepan with the vegetable broth.

Bring to the boil, then reduce the heat to low and simmer, partially covered, for 1 ½ hours.

Cool slightly, then blend in batches and season well with salt and pepper. Return to the saucepan and gently heat through.

Place in bowls and garnish with sour cream and dill.

Curried Parsnip Soup

Serves 4

Ingredients:

1.5 lb parsnips, peeled, chopped

2 onions, chopped

1 garlic clove

3 tbsp olive oil

1 tbs curry powder

½ cup heavy cream

salt and freshly ground pepper, to taste

Directions:

Sauté the onion and garlic together with the curry powder in a large saucepan. Stir in the parsnips and cook, stirring often, for 10 minutes. Add 6 cups of water, bring to the boil, and simmer for 30 minutes, or until the parsnips are tender.

Set aside to cool, then blend in batches until smooth. Return soup to pan over low heat and stir in the cream. Do not boil - only heat through. Season with salt and pepper.

Pumpkin and Bell Pepper Soup

Serves 4

Ingredients:

1 medium leek, chopped

9 oz pumpkin, peeled, deseeded, cut into small cubes

1 red pepper, cut into small pieces

1 can tomatoes, undrained, crushed

3 cups vegetable broth

½ tsp ground cumin

salt and black pepper, to taste

Directions:

Heat the olive oil in a medium saucepan and sauté the leek for 4-5 minutes. Add in the pumpkin and bell pepper and cook, stirring, for 5 minutes.

Add tomatoes, broth and cumin and bring to the boil. Cover, reduce heat to low and simmer, stirring occasionally, for 30 minutes or until the vegetables are soft.

Season with salt and pepper and leave aside to cool. Blend in batches and re-heat to serve.

Moroccan Pumpkin Soup

Serves 6

Ingredients:

1 leek, white part only, thinly sliced

3 cloves garlic, finely chopped

½ tsp ground ginger

½ tsp ground cinnamon

½ tsp ground cumin

2 carrots, peeled, coarsely chopped

2 lb pumpkin, peeled, deseeded, diced

1/3 cup chickpeas

5 tbsp olive oil

Juice of ½ lemon

1/2 cup finely cut parsley, to serve

Directions:

Heat oil in a large saucepan and gently sauté leek, garlic and 1/2 teaspoon of salt, stirring occasionally, until soft. Add in cinnamon, ginger and cumin and stir. Add carrots, pumpkin and chickpeas.

Stir in 5 cups of water and bring to the boil, then reduce heat and simmer for 50 minutes or until chickpeas are soft.

Remove from heat, add lemon juice, and blend in batches, until smooth. Return soup to the pan and cook, over low heat, stirring, for 4-5 minutes, or until heated through. Serve topped with parsley.

Spinach, Leek and Quinoa Soup

Serves 6

Ingredients:

½ cup quinoa

2 leeks halved lengthwise and sliced

1 onion, chopped

2 garlic cloves, chopped

1 tbsp olive oil

1 can of diced tomatoes, undrained

2 cups fresh spinach, chopped

6 cups vegetable broth

salt and pepper, to taste

Directions:

Heat a large soup pot over medium heat. Add olive oil and onion and gently sauté for 2 minutes. Add leeks and cook for another 2-3 minutes, then add in garlic and cook for a minute, until just fragrant.

Season with salt and pepper to taste. Add in the vegetable broth, canned tomatoes and quinoa. Bring to a boil then reduce heat and simmer for 10 minutes. Stir in the spinach and cook for another 5 minutes.

Vegetable Quinoa Soup

Serves 5-6

Ingredients:

½ cup quinoa

1 onion, chopped

1 potato, diced

1 carrot, diced

1 red bell pepper, chopped

2 tomatoes, chopped

1 zucchini, diced

1 tsp dried oregano

3-4 tbsp olive oil

black pepper, to taste

4 cups water

1 tbsp fresh lemon juice

Directions:

Rinse quinoa very well in a fine mesh strainer under running water; set aside to drain.

Heat the oil in a large soup pot and gently sauté the onions and carrot for 2-3 minutes, stirring every now and then. Add in the potato, bell pepper, tomatoes, spices and water. Stir to combine.

Cover, bring to a boil, then lower heat and simmer for 10 minutes. Add in the quinoa and zucchini; cover and simmer for 15 minutes or until the vegetables are tender. Add in the lemon juice; stir to combine.

Broccoli and Potato Soup

Serves 4-5

Ingredients:

2 lb broccoli, cut into florets

2 potatoes, chopped

1 big onion, chopped

3 garlic cloves, crushed

4 cups water

1 tbsp olive oil

¼ tsp ground nutmeg

Directions:

Heat oil in a large saucepan over medium-high heat. Add in onion and garlic and sauté, stirring, for 3 minutes or until soft.

Add broccoli, potato and 4 cups of cold water. Cover and bring to the boil, then reduce heat to low. Simmer, stirring, for 10 to 15 minutes, or until the potato is tender.

Remove from heat. Blend until smooth. Return to pan. Cook for 5 minutes or until heated through. Season with nutmeg and pepper before serving.

Creamy Potato Soup

Serves 4-5

Ingredients:

4-5 medium potatoes, peeled and cut into small cubes

2 carrots, chopped

1 zucchini, chopped

1 celery rib, chopped

3 cups water

3 tbsp olive oil

1 cup whole milk

½ tsp dried rosemary

salt, to taste

black pepper, to taste

a bunch of fresh parsley for garnish, finely cut

Directions:

Heat the olive oil over medium heat and sauté the vegetables for 2-3 minutes. Add 3 cups of water and rosemary and bring the soup to a boil, then lower heat and simmer until all the vegetables are tender.

Blend the soup in a blender until smooth. Add a cup of warm milk and blend some more.

Serve warm, seasoned with black pepper and parsley sprinkled over each serving.

Leek, Rice and Potato Soup

Serves 4-5

Ingredients:

1/3 cup rice

4 cups of water

2-3 potatoes, diced

1 small onion, cut

1 leek halved lengthwise and sliced

3 tbsp olive oil

lemon juice, to serve

Directions:

Heat a soup pot over medium heat. Add olive oil and onion and sauté for 2 minutes. Add leeks and potatoes and cook for a few minutes more, stirring.

Add three cups of water, bring to a boil, reduce heat and simmer for 5 minutes. Add the very well washed rice and simmer for 10 minutes. Serve with lemon juice to taste.

Carrot and Chickpea Soup

Serves 4-5

Ingredients:

3-4 big carrots, chopped

1 leek, chopped

4 cups vegetable broth

1 cup canned chickpeas, undrained

½ cup orange juice

2 tbsp olive oil

½ tsp cumin

½ tsp ginger

4-5 tbsp yogurt, to serve

Directions:

Heat oil in a large saucepan over medium heat. Add leek and carrots and sauté until soft. Add orange juice, broth, chickpeas and spices. Bring to the boil.

Reduce heat to medium-low and simmer, covered, for 15 minutes. Blend soup until smooth, return to pan. Season with salt and pepper.

Stir over heat until heated through. Pour in 4-5 bowls, top with yogurt and serve.

Sweet Potato Soup

Serves 6-7

Ingredients:

2 lb sweet potato, peeled, chopped

1 lb potatoes, peeled chopped

1 medium onions, chopped

4 cups chicken broth

5 tbsp olive oil

2 cloves garlic, minced

1 red chili pepper, finely chopped

salt and pepper, to taste

½ cup heavy cream

Directions:

Heat the olive oil in a large pot over medium heat and sauté the onions, garlic and chili pepper until just fragrant. Add the potatoes and sweet potatoes and add in the chicken broth. Bring to a boil.

Reduce heat to low and simmer 30 minutes or until potatoes are tender. Transfer the soup to a blender or food processor and blend, until smooth. Return to the pot and continue cooking for a few more minutes. Remove soup from heat; stir in the cream.

Irish Carrot Soup

Serves 5-6

Ingredients:

5-6 carrots, peeled, chopped

2 potatoes, peeled, chopped

1 small onion, chopped

4 cups chicken broth

3 tbsp olive oil

salt and pepper, to taste

1 cup sour cream, to serve

Directions:

Heat olive oil in a deep saucepan over medium-high heat and sauté the onion and carrot until tender. Add in potatoes and chicken broth.

Bring to the boil then reduce heat and simmer, partially covered, for 30 minutes, or until carrots are tender.

Set aside to cool then blend in batches until smooth. Return soup to saucepan and cook, stirring, for 4-5 minutes, or until heated through.

Season with salt and pepper and serve with a dollop of cream.

Spicy Carrot Soup

Serves 6-7

Ingredients:

10 carrots, peeled and chopped

2 medium onions, chopped

4-5 cups water

5 tbsp olive oil

2 cloves garlic, minced

1 big red chili pepper, finely chopped

½ bunch, fresh coriander, finely cut

salt and pepper to taste

½ cup heavy cream

Directions:

Heat the olive oil in a large pot over medium heat and sauté the onions, carrots, garlic and chili pepper until tender. Add 4-5 cups of water and bring to a boil.

Reduce heat to low and simmer 30 minutes. Transfer the soup to a blender or food processor and blend, until smooth. Return to the pot and continue cooking for a few more minutes.

Remove soup from heat; stir in the cream. Serve with coriander sprinkled over each serving.

Lentil, Barley and Mushroom Soup

Serves 4-5

Ingredients:

2 medium leeks, trimmed, halved, sliced

10 white mushrooms, sliced

3 garlic cloves, cut

2 bay leaves

2 cans tomatoes, chopped, undrained

3/4 cup red lentils

1/3 cup barley

3 tbsp olive oil

1 tsp paprika

1 tsp savory

½ tsp cumin

Directions:

Heat oil in a large saucepan over medium-high heat. Sauté leeks and mushrooms for 3 to 4 minutes or until softened. Add cumin, paprika, savory and tomatoes, lentils, barley, and 5 cups of cold water. Season with salt and pepper. Cover and bring to the boil.

Reduce heat to low. Simmer for 35 to 40 minutes, or until barley is tender.

Mushroom Soup

Serves 4

Ingredients:

2 cups mushrooms, peeled and chopped

1 onion, chopped

2 cloves of garlic, crushed and chopped

1 tsp dried thyme

3 cups vegetable broth

salt and pepper, to taste

3 tbsp olive oil

Directions:

Sauté onions and garlic in a large soup pot until transparent. Add thyme and mushrooms.

Cook for 10 minutes then add the vegetable broth and simmer for another 10-20 minutes. Blend, season and serve.

Mediterranean Chickpea Soup

Serves 9-10

Ingredients:

2 cups canned chickpeas, drained

a bunch of spring onions, finely cut

2 cloves garlic, crushed

1 cup canned tomatoes, diced

4 cups vegetable broth

3 tbsp olive oil

1 bay leaf

½ tsp rosemary

½ cup freshly grated Parmesan cheese

Directions:

Sauté onion and garlic in olive oil in a heavy soup pot. Add broth, chickpeas, tomatoes, bay leaf and rosemary.

Bring to the boil, then reduce heath and simmer for 20 minutes.

Remove from heat and serve sprinkled with Parmesan cheese.

French Vegetable Soup

Serves 4-5

Ingredients:

1 leek, thinly sliced

1 large zucchini, peeled and diced

1 cup green beans, cut

2 garlic cloves, cut

4 cups vegetable broth

1 cup canned tomatoes, chopped

3.5 oz vermicelli, broken into small pieces

3 tbsp olive oil

black pepper to taste

4 tbsp freshly grated Parmesan cheese

Directions:

Sauté the leek, zucchini, green beans and garlic for about 5 minutes. Add the vegetable broth. Stir in the tomatoes and bring to the boil, then reduce heat.

Add black pepper to taste and simmer for 10 minutes, or until the vegetables are tender but still holding their shape.

Stir in the vermicelli. Cover again and simmer for a further 5 minutes. Serve warm sprinkled with Parmesan cheese.

Minted Pea Soup

Serves 4

Ingredients:

1 onion, finely chopped

2 garlic cloves, finely chopped

4 cups vegetable broth

1/3 cup mint leaves

2 lb green peas, frozen

3 tbsp olive oil

1/4 cup yogurt, to serve

small mint leaves, to serve

Directions:

Heat oil in a large saucepan over medium-high heat and sauté onion and garlic for 5 minutes or until soft.

Add vegetable broth and bring to the boil, then add mint and peas. Cover, reduce heat, and cook for 3 minutes, or until peas are tender but still green. Remove from heat.

Set aside to cool slightly, then blend soup, in batches, until smooth. Return soup to saucepan over medium-low heat and cook until heated through. Season with salt and pepper. Serve topped with yogurt, pepper and mint leaves.

Brown Lentil Soup

Serves 8-9

Ingredients:

2 cups brown lentils

2 onions, chopped

5-6 cloves garlic, peeled

3 medium carrots, chopped

2-3 medium tomatoes, ripe

6 cups water

4 tbsp olive oil

1 ½ tsp paprika

1 tsp summer savory

Directions:

Heat oil in a deep soup pot, add the onions and carrots and sauté until golden. Add in paprika and lentils with 6 cups of warm water.

Bring to the boil, lower heat and simmer for 30 minutes. Chop the tomatoes and add them to the soup, together with garlic and summer savory.

Cook for 15 more minutes, add salt to taste and serve.

Moroccan Lentil Soup

Serves 8-9

Ingredients:

1 cup red lentils

1/2 cup canned chickpeas, drained

2 onions, chopped

2 cloves garlic, minced

1 cup canned tomatoes, chopped

1/2 cup canned white beans, drained

3 carrots, diced

3 celery ribs, diced

6 cups water

1 tsp ginger, grated

1 tsp ground cardamom

½ tsp ground cumin

3 tbsp olive oil

Directions:

In a large pot, sauté onions, garlic and ginger in olive oil, for about 5 minutes. Add the water, lentils, chickpeas, white beans, tomatoes, carrots, celery, cardamom and cumin.

Bring to a boil for a few minutes, then simmer for ½ hour or longer, until the lentils are tender.

Puree half the soup in a food processor or blender. Return the pureed soup to the pot, stir and serve.

White Bean Soup

Serves: 6

Ingredients:

1 cup white beans

2-3 carrots

2 onions, finely chopped

1-2 tomatoes, grated

1 red bell pepper, chopped

4-5 springs of fresh mint and parsley

1 tsp paprika

3 tbsp sunflower oil

salt

Directions:

Soak the beans in cold water for 3-4 hours, drain and discard the water.

Cover the beans with cold water. Add the oil, finely chopped carrots, onions and pepper. Bring to the boil and simmer until the beans are tender. Add the grated tomatoes, mint, paprika and salt.

Simmer for another 15 minutes. Serve sprinkled with finely chopped parsley.

Tomato Soup

Serves: 5-6

Ingredients:

5 cups chopped fresh tomatoes or 28 oz canned tomatoes

1/3 cup rice

3 cups water

1 large onion, diced

4 garlic cloves, minced

3 tbsp olive oil

1 tsp salt

1 tbsp paprika

1 tsp sugar

½ bunch fresh parsley, to serve

Directions:

Sauté onions and garlic in oil, in a large soup pot. When the onions have softened, add in tomatoes, stir in paprika and mix well to coat vegetables.

Bring to a boil, lower heat, and simmer for 15 minutes. Blend the soup, then return to the pot, add water and rice, a teaspoon of sugar, and bring to the boil again.

Simmer for 15 minutes stirring occasionally. Sprinkle with parsley and serve.

Cauliflower Soup

Serves 4-5

Ingredients:

1 large onion, finely cut

1 medium head cauliflower, chopped

2-3 garlic cloves, minced

4 cups water

½ cup whole cream

4 tbsp olive oil

salt, to taste

fresh ground black pepper, to taste

Directions:

Heat the olive oil in a large pot over medium heat and sauté the onion, cauliflower and garlic. Stir in the water and bring the soup to a boil.

Reduce heat, cover, and simmer for 40 minutes. Remove the soup from heat, add the cream and blend in a blender. Season with salt and pepper.

Creamy Artichoke Soup

Serves 4

Ingredients:

1 can artichoke hearts, drained

3 cups vegetable broth

2 tbsp lemon juice

1 small onion, finely cut

2 cloves garlic, crushed

3 tbsp olive oil

2 tbsp flour

½ cup heavy cream

Directions:

Gently sauté the onion and garlic in some olive oil. Add the flour, whisking constantly, and then add the hot vegetable broth slowly, while still whisking. Cook for about 5 minutes.

Blend the artichoke, lemon juice, salt and pepper until smooth. Add the puree to the broth mix, stir well, and then stir in the cream. Cook until heated through. Garnish with a swirl of cream or a sliver of artichoke.

Tomato Artichoke Soup

Serves 4

Ingredients:

1 can artichoke hearts, drained

1 can diced tomatoes, undrained

3 cups vegetable broth

1 small onion, chopped

2 cloves garlic, crushed

1 tbsp pesto

black pepper, to taste

Directions:

Combine all ingredients in the slow cooker.

Cover and cook on low for 8-10 hours or on high for 4-5 hours.

Blend the soup in batches and return it to the slow cooker. Season with salt and pepper to taste and serve.

Roasted Red Pepper Soup

Serves 5-6

Ingredients:

5-6 red peppers

1 large onion, chopped

2 garlic cloves, crushed

4 medium tomatoes, chopped

4 cups vegetable broth

3 tbsp olive oil

2 bay leaves

Directions:

Grill the peppers or roast them in the oven at 400 F until the skins are a little burnt. Place the roasted peppers in a brown paper bag or a lidded container and leave covered for about 10 minutes. This makes it easier to peel them. Peel the skins and remove the seeds. Cut the peppers in small pieces.

Heat oil in a large saucepan over medium-high heat. Add onion and garlic and sauté, stirring, for 3 minutes or until onion has softened. Add the red peppers, bay leaves, tomato and simmer for 5 minutes.

Add in broth. Season with pepper. Bring to the boil, then reduce heat and simmer for 20 more minutes. Set aside to cool slightly. Blend, in batches, until smooth and serve.

Vietnamese Noodle Soup

Serves 4

Ingredients:

9 oz rice stick noodles

4 cups vegetable broth

1 lemongrass stem, only pale part, finely chopped

2 garlic cloves, cut

½ tsp ground ginger

1 long red chili, thinly sliced

3.5 oz shiitake mushrooms

1 cup bean sprouts

4 tbsp lime juice

coriander and mint leaves, to garnish

Directions:

Pour boiling water over the noodles and leave aside for 10 minutes, or until soft.

Place the vegetable broth, lemongrass, garlic, ginger, chili and 3 cups of water in a large saucepan. Bring to the boil, then reduce heat to medium. Simmer for 10 minutes.

Add mushrooms and cook for 5 more minutes, then stir in the lime juice.

Divide the noodles and bean sprouts among bowls. Serve the soup topped with coriander and mint leaves.

Spinach, Nettle and Feta Cheese Soup

Serves 6

Ingredients:

1 lb frozen spinach, thawed

13 oz nettles, young top shoots

3.5 oz feta cheese

1 large onion or 4-5 scallions

2 -3 tbsp light cream

3-4 tbsp olive oil

¼ cup white rice

1-2 cloves garlic

4 cups water

salt and black pepper, to taste

Directions:

Clean the young nettles, wash and cook them in slightly salted water. Drain, rinse, drain again, chop them and leave aside.

Heat the oil in a soup pot, add the onion, garlic and paprika and sauté for a few minutes, stirring constantly. Remove from heat.

Add the spinach and nettles. Add about 4 cups of hot water and season with salt and pepper. Bring back to the boil, then reduce the heat and simmer for around 30 minutes.

In the meantime crumble the cheese with a fork. When the soup is ready stir in the crumbled feta cheese and the cream. Serve hot.

Nettle Soup

Serves 6

Ingredients:

1.5 lb young top shoots of nettles, well washed

3-4 tbsp sunflower oil

2 potatoes, peeled and diced small

1 bunch spring onions, coarsely chopped

3 cups hot water

1 tsp salt

Directions:

Clean the young nettles, wash and cook them in slightly salted water. Drain, rinse, drain again and then chop or pass through a sieve.

Sauté the chopped spring onions and potatoes in the oil until the potatoes start to color a little. Turn off the heat, add the nettles, then gradually stir in the water. Stir well, then simmer until the potatoes are cooked through.

Gazpacho

Serves 6-7

Ingredients:

2.25 lb tomatoes, peeled and halved

1 onion, sliced

1 green pepper, sliced

1 big cucumber, peeled and sliced

2 cloves garlic

salt to taste

4 tbsp olive oil

1 tbsp apple cider vinegar

to garnish

½ onion, chopped

1 green pepper, chopped

1 cucumber, chopped

Directions:

Place the tomatoes, garlic, onion, green pepper, cucumber, salt, olive oil and vinegar in a blender or food processor and puree until smooth, adding small amounts of cold water if needed to achieve desired consistency.

Serve the gazpacho chilled with the chopped onion, green pepper and cucumber.

Cold Cucumber Soup

Serves 4

Ingredients:

1 large or two small cucumbers

2 cups yogurt

4-5 cloves garlic, crushed or chopped

1 cup cold water

4 tbsp sunflower or olive oil

2 bunches of fresh dill, finely chopped

½ cup crushed walnuts

Directions:

Wash the cucumber, peel and cut into small cubes.

In a large bowl dilute the yogurt with water to taste, add the cucumber and garlic, stirring well.

Add salt to the taste, garnish with the dill and the crushed walnuts and put in the fridge to cool.

FREE BONUS RECIPES: 20 Superfood Paleo and Vegan Smoothies for Vibrant Health and Easy Weight Loss

Winter Greens Smoothie

Serves: 2

Prep time: 5 min

Ingredients:

2 broccoli florets, frozen

1½ cup coconut water

½ banana

½ cup pineapple

1 cup fresh spinach

2 kale leaves

Directions:

Combine ingredients in blender and blend until smooth. Enjoy!

Delicious Kale Smoothie

Serves: 2

Prep time: 5 min

Ingredients:

2-3 ice cubes

1½ cup apple juice

3-4 kale leaves

1 apple, cut

1 cup strawberries

½ tsp cloves

Directions:

Combine ingredients in blender and purée until smooth.

Cherry Smoothie

Serves: 2

Prep time: 5 min

Ingredients:

2-3 ice cubes

1½ cup almond or coconut milk

1½ cup pitted and frozen cherries

½ avocado

1 tsp cinnamon

1 tsp chia seeds

Directions :

Combine all ingredients into a blender and process until smooth. Enjoy!

Banana and Coconut Smoothie

Serves: 2

Prep time: 5 min

Ingredients:

1 frozen banana, chopped

1½ cup coconut water

2-3 small broccoli florets

1 tbsp coconut butter

Directions :

Add all ingredients into a blender and blend until the smoothie turns into an even and smooth consistency. Enjoy!

Avocado and Pineapple Smoothie

Serves: 2

Prep time: 5 min

Ingredients:

3-4 ice cubes

1½ cup coconut water

½ avocado

2 cups diced pineapple

Directions:

Combine all ingredients in a blender, and blend until smooth. Enjoy!

Carrot and Mango Smoothie

Serves: 2

Prep time: 5 min

Ingredients:

1 cup frozen mango chunks

1 cup carrot juice

½ cup orange juice

1 carrot, chopped

1 tsp chia seeds

1 tsp grated ginger

Directions:

Combine all ingredients in a blender, and blend until smooth. Enjoy!

Strawberry and Coconut Smoothie

Serves: 2

Prep time: 5 min

Ingredients:

3-4 ice cubes

1½ cup coconut milk

2 cups fresh strawberries

1 tsp chia seeds

Directions:

Place all ingredients in a blender and purée until smooth. Enjoy!

Beautiful Skin Smoothie

Serves: 2

Prep time: 5 min

Ingredients:

1 cup frozen strawberries

1½ cup green tea

1 peach, chopped

½ avocado

5-6 raw almonds

1 tsp coconut oil

Directions:

Place all ingredients in a blender and purée until smooth. Enjoy!

Kiwi and Pear Smoothie

Serves: 2

Prep time: 5 min

Ingredients:

1 frozen banana, chopped

3 oranges, juiced

2 kiwi, peeled and halved

1 pear, chopped

1 tbsp coconut butter

Directions:

Juice oranges and combine all ingredients in a blender then blend until smooth. Enjoy!

Tropical Smoothie

Serves: 2

Prep time: 5 min

Ingredients:

2-3 ice cubes

1½ cup coconut water

½ avocado

1 mango, peeled, diced

1 cup pineapple, chopped

2-3 dates, pitted

Directions:

Place all ingredients in a blender and purée until smooth. Enjoy!

Melon Smoothie

Serves: 2

Prep time: 5 min

Ingredients:

1 frozen banana, chopped

1-2 frozen broccoli florets

1 cup coconut water

½ honeydew melon, cut in pieces

1 tsp chia seeds

Directions:

Combine all ingredients in a blender, and blend until smooth.

Healthy Skin Smoothie

Serves: 2

Prep time: 5 min

Ingredients:

1 cup frozen berries

1 cup almond milk

½ avocado

1 pear

1 tbsp ground pumpkin seeds

1 tsp vanilla extract

Directions :

Put all ingredients in a blender and blend until smooth. Enjoy!

Paleo Dessert Smoothie

Serves: 2

Prep time: 5 min

Ingredients:

1 frozen banana

1 cup coconut water

1 cup raspberries

2 apricots, chopped

1 tbsp almond butter

Directions:

Put all ingredients into blender. Blend until smooth. Enjoy!

Easy Superfood Smoothie

Serves: 2

Prep time: 5 min

Ingredients:

3-4 ice cubes

1½ cup green tea

1 pear, chopped

½ cup blueberries

½ cup blackberries

1 tbsp almond butter

Directions :

Place all ingredients in a blender and blend for until even. Enjoy!

Antioxidant Smoothie

Serves: 2

Prep time: 5 min

Ingredients:

1 cup frozen raspberries

1½ cups orange juice

2 kiwi, peeled and halved

1 tsp chia seeds

1 tsp ground pumpkin seeds

Directions:

Blend all ingredients in a blender until smooth. Enjoy!

Coconut and Date Smoothie

Serves: 2

Prep time: 5 min

Ingredients:

1 frozen banana, chopped

1½ cup coconut milk

2 leaves kale

15 dates, pitted

Directions:

Combine all ingredients in a blender and blend until smooth. Enjoy!

Kiwi and Grapefruit Smoothie

Serves: 2

Prep time: 5 min

Ingredients:

3-4 ice cubes

1½ cup grapefruit juice

1 banana, chopped

2 kiwi, cut

1 tsp sunflower seeds

Directions:

Juice the grapefruit then combine with the ice, kiwi and banana. Add a teaspoon of sunflower seeds and blend until smooth. Enjoy!

Mango and Nectarine Smoothie

Serves: 2

Prep time: 5 min

Ingredients:

3-4 ice cubes

1 cup almond milk

1 mango, peeled, diced

3 nectarines, chopped

1 tbsp ground flaxseed

Directions:

Put all ingredients into blender. Blend until smooth. Enjoy!

Pineapple Smoothie

Serves: 2

Prep time: 5 min

Ingredients:

2-3 ice cubes

2-3 oranges, juiced

2 cups pineapple, chopped

1 carrot, chopped

1 tbsp ground pumpkin seeds

1 tsp grated ginger

Directions:

Juice the oranges then combine with ice, carrot and pineapple in a blender. Add the pumpkin seeds ginger and blend until smooth. Enjoy!

Easy Vitamin Smoothie

Serves: 2

Prep time: 5 min

Ingredients:

2-3 ice cubes

2 pink grapefruits, juiced

½ avocado

1 carrot, chopped

1 cup strawberries

3-4 dates, pitted

Directions:

Juice the grapefruit then combine with ice and other ingredients. Blend until smooth. Enjoy!

About the Author

Vesela lives in Bulgaria with her family of six (including the Jack Russell Terrier). Her passion is going green in everyday life and she loves to prepare homemade cosmetic and beauty products for all her family and friends.

Vesela has been publishing her cookbooks for over a year now. If you want to see other healthy family recipes that she has published, together with some natural beauty books, you can check out her Author Page on Amazon.

Printed in Poland
by Amazon Fulfillment
Poland Sp. z o.o., Wrocław